Week/
End

Week/
End

Sarah Duncan

HEADMISTRESS PRESS

ISBN 978-0-9987610-3-9

Cover illustration © Nikki McClure.
Cover & book design by Mary Meriam.

PUBLISHER
Headmistress Press
60 Shipview Lane
Sequim, WA 98382
Telephone: 917-428-8312
Email: headmistresspress@gmail.com
Website: headmistresspress.blogspot.com

this book is 4 lonely queers everywhere
&
lm

I. ebb

Where would you like to sleep tonight? You asked, trying to sound chamomile. I stirred.

We'd planned that I'd stay in your old apartment.
But days before I boarded the plane, we decided it was too far away from your new house.
So, here I was in your new kitchen; your something to my something.
We'd met over a year ago,
right before we were both leaving
another city for our lives. Without looking,
we'd grabbed love off the coat rack on the way out the door,
hoping.

I'd like to stay in your bed, I offered
as if it was a question, which it was, which it wasn't.

Okay, you said, sharp with worry.

Anything could have traveled between us:
a family of four in a station wagon,
the very first pride parade, all of last year,
a roving, benevolent gang of cyclists, 3,000 metaphors for silence.

I kept my chin hooked to my chest because I was afraid, the absent noise
like midnight trumpets at the end
of the world.
Guilty, you reached across the mattress to stroke my head.

My whole body closed its eyes.
I imagined inflating
your hand so I could roll, small and entire,
into your palm's heat even while the rest of you was cold.

I fled your room for another.

The water pressure has been really inconsistent, your housemate said to us the next day,
her hands in the sink of your new house. *Have you noticed?*

She told us that sometimes, the water all but stops at first, and then rushes out.
Other times, the water comes out in a slow glide towards normal.
Other others, it's a trickle, all but there.
No, I haven't noticed, you said.

It was evening. You were standing away from me, arms tugging
themselves across your chest. Earlier, we'd stopped to hug each other in the middle of the
sidewalk, like we were practicing. Earlier, we'd talked about the elephant
that appears when we name the elephant.
Earlier, you'd asked to hold my hand.
Yes, I've noticed, I said, unsure which one of us was lying.

I noticed a struck match in your toilet bowl. You told me it was a "Canadian thing," to hide the smell of defecation. The match is lit, waved in order to dispel, then dropped. In the few days following, I avoided using the matches out of loyalty to a sulky definition of authenticity, a self-righteous refusal of panglossian ideologies:

Shit stinks. Why avoid it?

Eventually, I tried it. It took me several strikes to light the match.

We went to an aquarium. Tanks of identical fish the size of our feet moved their mouths
in synchronicity. *If you had to be any fish, what kind would you be?*
I hate this game, you replied. In the tunnel,
our feet twisted with the floor and sharks scowled death above, watching us dip
muddy fists into each other's gravel mouths, like miners,
sifting for any flecks of valuable yellow.

I crawled into an arched fish tank and posed, feigning.
Oh trapped among the trapped!
I stood, accidentally rapping my skull on the glass,
— and you briefly laughed,
hard as a body overboard, hitting the salt.

Was that the gold?

We went to a farmer's market. Walking beside you, I ate my tongue and spat out the seeds.
You picked up the ones you could see, examined them for what they were:
sparse words, cracked. Unusable,
you gave them back. All day
we did this. Defeated, you
bought rhubarb at the market and I trailed behind in my sulk
and summer dress while you swayed around passerby.
I could see the weight of me on top of you,
your hope smoking
and sunken.

1.

How do you want me to tell it?
The day and I had talked long.
I'd let the sun convince me to swap
demand for offer, beat for beam.
I'd greeted you ready to grow you a bright balloon.

You and the day had also talked long.
You'd let fluorescent bulbs lure you into parables of unrelenting.
You'd let cold bodies sing about what it means to be unsalvageable.
You returned from work in your white coat and handed me an official notice
with a written prescription: it's time.

2.

Or,
should I say we were boiling? That we would either overrun or scorch?
Should I say I pulled the fit from my hair and threw it at you?
That you pulled stones from your sleeves and stacked them between us?
That you peeked over and told me if I kept the keening up, you'd build another one?
That you urged me to admire the salted smoothness?

3.

I wrote O K on the notice and pushed it through a cut in your rocks.
I heard you take the paper and fold it.
I heard you tie your shoes.

Who do you see? I asked you.
I see the door, you said.

What is my name? Which of the letters have been your favorite?
I hate this game, you said.

4.

How do you want me to tell it?
Should I say it was time?

II. flow

We decided to go camping, because

we wanted to sing old dirges under old trees because

I wanted soft space with you, shadow intimacy because

you wanted to give me a memorial something, remain honest.

Wet, we crawled into your tent. Curling up,

like the first night, to curl away. Across

the campsite was a midnight orchestra, tuning.

The scales, the whistles of reeds, spit in the horns, grease keys.

Are you warm enough? We buried ourselves

under light nylon cloth, watched it pucker and cave as the clouds sung their fury down,

an elegy, *sorry*—

sorry, a masterpiece.

We decided to come back early, because

the shore skies too much resembled a mirror, because

our throats had split and our lips were sponge, because

we wanted to mop up, wring out, part.

We beached on your couch. *I won't sleep tonight*

unless I'm piss drunk, I swore. So we drank

shots of cacti that tasted like forest fire and absolution,

talked each other into cracking. Creaking, edging, I asked you

to come in. *What's one more time?*

You swung closed, latched, left me

leaning against the white wall,

punishing myself.

Using the knives of my nails, I picked at

my left arm, digging a moat in my own skin.

I could wrap my shame in a burlap sack and drown it

here, I thought. I could feed it to a swarm of alligators, to looming sharks,

to violently beautiful jellyfish, to someone

who wasn't me or you. I could blot out the last few days.

I could cover this trip in a red shroud, I could pray. I could hang

it in a room with high ceilings and say look at how it looks: like living,

like mess, like color, like sting.

I watched the blood pool and hug itself, a tiny red

mushroom cloud, blanketing the town—cells—around it.

I bombed myself. I was surprised. It was easy.

That first night after I'd moved into the hostel, I decimated sailboats, the sides of summer homes. Threw my branches around the room, smashing. Shredded nests of birds. Churned air to make a deadly water. Swallowed pounds of dirt. Ate my own roots. I ripped my leaves off and used them to cover my eyes. I ripped my leaves off and balled them and threw them at you. I ripped my leaves off and stuffed them into my cunt and pretended they were your fingers. I ripped my leaves off and laid down on the plastic twin bed. I bled sap and chlorophyll onto thin white sheets until I

fell

     asleep.

The second night in the hostel, I fumbled for my body's button. Click. Out came a torrent

of dead crows, wet and pearl eyed. Flopping out over my thighs, they birthed themselves,

omens weighing the mattress with graves. I curled my hands toward one

slumped against my calf. This bird. These birds. *These birds*

used to sing, I said. I pulled more sticky feathers

from my between. *These birds used to fly.* Too, too long

inside.

The third night in the hostel, I peeled a clove of garlic in the middle of the night.

Gasped until it became a laugh. The windows pressed me

until I wrote on glass in chilled block letters

H E L P & F U C K & U

Why didn't you warn me?

Why didn't you tell me to pack a hat and gloves?

And that they'd need to both be black?

The last evening, we met at a bar in the city, like everyone else in the city.

You asked me if I regretted this trip.

I sat for a moment, rolling this around my tongue.

I thought about how I can count the times you've cried in front of me on one hand.

During my poetry reading; one finger.

The day of your graduation, as you read what I'd written about who I'd found you to be—

whole, strong, a planter of your own promise; two fingers.

Holding each other in the rental car, days before this conversation,

when I'd felt a wet spot above my ear and I could only guess that you might be crying,

quickly, invisibly, because I wasn't

looking; three fingers.

I'm afraid, you continued, holding out another offering, *that without giving romance[1],*

I won't have anything to give you that you want.

We break so differently, I thought.

---

[1] Reader, there is another. Another lover: new, handsome, hers. I won't bring him into this, even though he hovered above all our hours on this visit, even though she shutters when she talks about him, even though she appears to be peeling off the petals with the fragrant kick and bloom, the ones I liked most when I met her. She crosses my heart and swears on hers that his hands are in his own pockets, and what can I do but take her word for it? Yes. There is another. I won't put him in this, except to leave him here, except to say that he is.

Near the end of the trip, we had dinner with your parents.

On my way to meet you there, it rained. Pedestrians cursed bloated sneakers, ruined

phones in mushy pockets, paddled themselves out

of the street into cement shelters. A cove

I found smelled like urine, which means

it smelled like New York, where we'd met.

I wish I could smash those memories, you'd told me on some

other, separate day, hurt and tired of me clutching

those old damn photographs,

expecting you to constantly emulate them.

The pee smell was coming from me; I'd sat in it.

I placed my hands

against my denim back pocket: sticky. I gagged. I stuck

my hands into the rain, watching the water

ballet off my fingers. *This goddamn week of water. This goddamn*

dirt. This goddamn piss and shit and relief.

The last evening at the altar of the bar you paid for my cider, bowing your head.

I understood. You were not praying, you were sinking.

I almost said I'm sorry but I know.

You asked again.

Q: *Was it still worth coming?*

On our last morning, we found a diner with an open back booth.

I sat across from you and we winced.

I said I'd miss your parents, and your brother,

and you winced,

your face, unforgettable

on our last morning, crinkling

like wrapping paper. Embarrassed, I folded

my face.

You asked me what happened to my arm and I winced and I told you

the only lie I've ever told you.

On our last morning, you believed me, you had to pay

for breakfast

on our last morning.

My debit card failed. *Do you want me*

to pay you back? No you shook

the *no* out of your head.

On our last morning, we walked back to your home.

I sobbed in your guest room

and you sighed.

You sat next to me and my zipped bags.

You told me you loved me

and for the first time

on our last

morning my throat closed instead of opened but

I turned toward the street I

turned away from you I   said   *See ya*

which means

                        A: *Yes*

About the Author

Sarah M. Duncan is a cis white queer dis/abled femme who spends her time as a writer, performer, grassroots organizer, teacher, Buffy fan, and academic. She recently graduated with an MFA from the University of Wyoming, where she studied poetry with an emphasis on critical race theory and queer studies. Currently, she lives in Jamaica Plain, Boston, where she is continuing her education at UMass Boston in American Studies. Her poetry has been published by The Racial Imaginary Institute, *Souvenir Lit Journal, Heavy Feather Review,* and the anthology *States of the Union,* among others. She has performed her poetry through New York City at spaces like La MaMa Experimental Theater and Dixon Place. Her plays "Come Back Up" and "Bees and Lions" have been produced by Sanguine Theatre Company NYC. *Week/End* was a semi-finalist for the 2018 Charlotte Mew Chapbook Prize and a finalist for the 2018 Yemassee Journal Chapbook Contest.

Seed - Janice Gould

The Princess of Pain - Carolyn Gage & Sudie Rakusin

She/Her/Hers - Amy Lauren

Spoiled Meat - Nicole Santalucia

Cake - Jen Rouse

The Salt and the Song - Virginia Petrucci

mad girl's crush tweet - summer jade leavitt

Saturn coming out of its Retrograde - Briana Roldan

i am this girl - gina marie bernard

Week/End - Sarah Duncan

My Girl's Green Jacket - Mary Meriam

Nuts in Nutland - Mary Meriam, Hannah Barrett

Lovely - Lesléa Newman

Teeth & Teeth - Robin Reagler

How Distant the City - Freesia McKee

Shopgirls - Marissa Higgins

Riddle - Diane Fortney

When She Woke She Was an Open Field - Hilary Brown

God With Us - Amy Lauren

A Crown of Violets - Renée Vivien tr. Samantha Pious

Fireworks in the Graveyard - Joy Ladin

Social Dance - Carolyn Boll

The Force of Gratitude - Janice Gould

Spine - Sarah Caulfield

I Wore the Only Garden I've Ever Grown - Kathryn Leland

Diatribe from the Library - Farrell Greenwald Brenner

Blind Girl Grunt - Constance Merritt

Acid and Tender - Jen Rouse

Beautiful Machinery - Wendy DeGroat

Odd Mercy - Gail Thomas

The Great Scissor Hunt - Jessica K. Hylton

A Bracelet of Honeybees - Lynn Strongin

Whirlwind @ Lesbos - Risa Denenberg
The Body's Alphabet - Ann Tweedy
First name Barbie last name Doll - Maureen Bocka
Heaven to Me - Abe Louise Young
Sticky - Carter Steinmann
Tiger Laughs When You Push - Ruth Lehrer
Night Ringing - Laura Foley
Paper Cranes - Dinah Dietrich
On Loving a Saudi Girl - Carina Yun
The Burn Poems - Lynn Strongin
I Carry My Mother - Lesléa Newman
Distant Music - Joan Annsfire
The Awful Suicidal Swans - Flower Conroy
Joy Street - Laura Foley
Chiaroscuro Kisses - G.L. Morrison
The Lillian Trilogy - Mary Meriam
Lady of the Moon - Amy Lowell, Lillian Faderman, Mary Meriam
Irresistible Sonnets - ed. Mary Meriam
Lavender Review - ed. Mary Meriam

www.ingramcontent.com/pod-product-compliance
Lightning Source LLC
Chambersburg PA
CBHW081540040426
42447CB00014B/3441